# THE MUSCULAR SYSTEM

EARLY BIRD
BODY SYSTEMS

## BY REBECCA L. JOHNSON

LERNER PUBLICATIONS COMPANY • MINNEAPOLIS

Text copyright © 2005 by Rebecca L. Johnson

Lerner Publications Company
A division of Lerner Publishing Group
241 First Avenue North
Minneapolis, MN 55401 U.S.A.

Website address: www.lernerbook.com

Library of Congress Cataloging-in-Publication Data

Johnson, Rebecca L.
    The muscular system / by Rebecca L. Johnson.
       p.    cm.—(Early bird body systems)
    Includes index.
    ISBN: 0-8225-1248-3 (lib. bdg. : alk. paper)
    1. Muscles—Juvenile literature. I. Title.
QP321.J545  2005                                        2004002541

Manufactured in the United States of America
1 2 3 4 5 6 – JR – 10 09 08 07 06 05

# CONTENTS

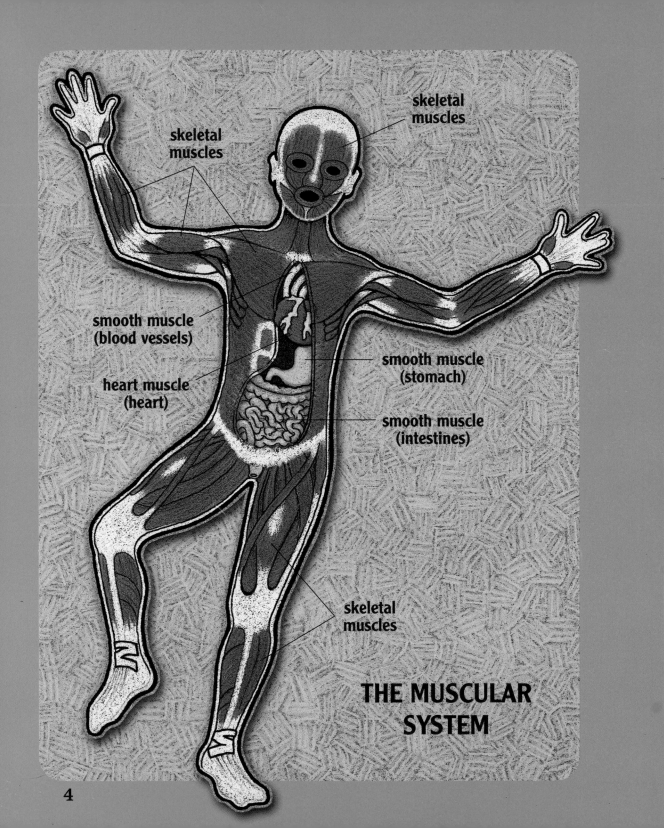

skeletal
muscles

skeletal
muscles

smooth muscle
(blood vessels)

heart muscle
(heart)

smooth muscle
(stomach)

smooth muscle
(intestines)

skeletal
muscles

**THE MUSCULAR
SYSTEM**

# BE A WORD DETECTIVE

Can you find these words as you read about the muscular system? Be a detective and try to figure out what they mean. You can turn to the glossary on page 46 for help.

biceps
blood vessels
brain
cells
contract
heart muscle

microscope
muscle fiber
nerves
nutrients
organs

oxygen
skeletal muscle
smooth muscle
tendons
triceps

# CHAPTER 1

# BODY MOVERS

What do muscles make it possible for you to do?

Every time you take a step, blink your eyes, or smile you can thank your muscles. Muscles make you move. Some movements are large. You leap over a puddle. You swing a bat. Other movements are small. You raise an eyebrow. You tap your finger.

You can see some muscles at work. Try "making a muscle" with your arm. Can you see the muscle bulging just under your skin?

**Some muscles you can see just under your skin.**

You can't see other muscles in your body. When you swallow, muscles push food into your stomach. Muscles in the stomach wall mix your food. Muscles in your heart move blood through your body.

**Swallowing involves muscles you can't see.**

**Muscles help you do all the things you do.**

You need your muscles for almost everything you do. So it's not surprising that you have hundreds of them. All these muscles make up your muscular system. The muscular system works with other body systems to keep you alive and healthy. It helps you do all the things you do.

**Picking up an apple uses muscles you can control.**

    You can control some muscles. You can make them move just by thinking. Suppose you want to pick up an apple. You reach out and curl your fingers around the apple. You lift it up. You decide you want to do this. And your muscles make it happen.

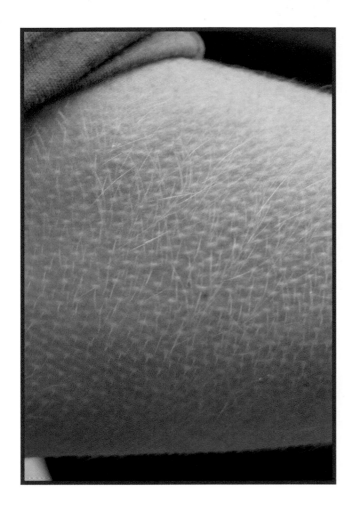

As hard as you try, you can't control the muscles that make goose bumps on your skin.

There are other muscles that you cannot control, no matter how hard you try. You can't make food travel to your stomach more quickly. You can't make your heart beat more slowly. These kinds of muscles do their work automatically.

All muscles are alike in one important way. They all can contract, or shorten. When a muscle contracts, it moves whatever body part it's attached to.

**By contracting, muscles make body parts move.**

When your biceps contracts, your lower arm bends up.

You can see muscles contract in your arm. The big muscle in your upper arm is called the biceps (BYE-sehps). When your biceps contracts, your lower arm moves up. Put your left hand on your right biceps. Bend your right elbow. Can you feel your biceps contracting as your lower arm moves up?

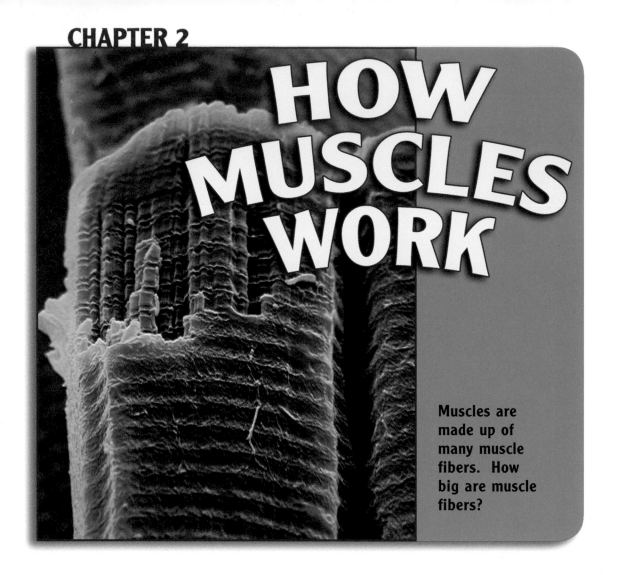

# CHAPTER 2

# HOW MUSCLES WORK

Muscles are made up of many muscle fibers. How big are muscle fibers?

Muscles move body parts by contracting. But how do muscles contract?

Muscles are made up of cells. Each muscle cell is called a muscle fiber. A muscle fiber is thinner than one of the hairs on your head.

Inside each muscle fiber are hundreds of strands. These strands are made up of even thinner strands. The thinnest strands overlap each other. They look like fingers laced together.

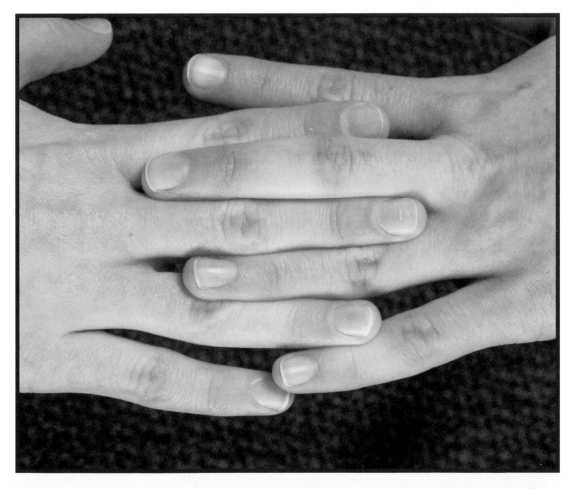

The thinnest strands of muscle fiber overlap like fingers laced together.

Your brain controls your body. It sends messages all the time. These messages go to every part of your body. They travel along nerves. Nerves reach into every muscle. They touch every muscle fiber.

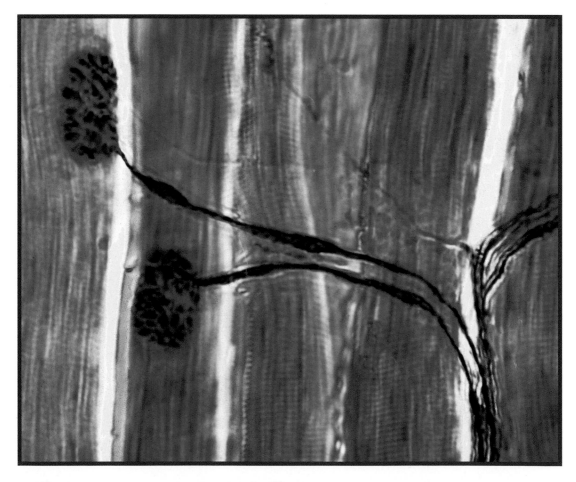

**Nerves carry messages to muscle fibers.**

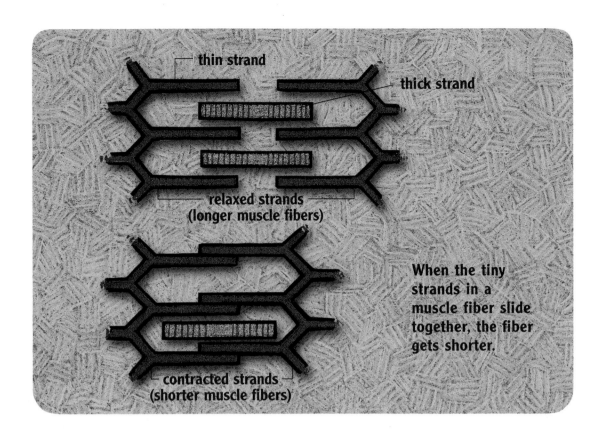

thin strand

thick strand

relaxed strands
(longer muscle fibers)

When the tiny strands in a muscle fiber slide together, the fiber gets shorter.

contracted strands
(shorter muscle fibers)

When a message reaches a muscle fiber, the tiny strands inside it move. The strands slide toward each other. So the muscle fiber gets shorter.

As muscle fibers get shorter, the whole muscle contracts. It pulls on the body parts that it is attached to. It makes the body parts move.

# CHAPTER 3

# MUSCLES YOU MOVE

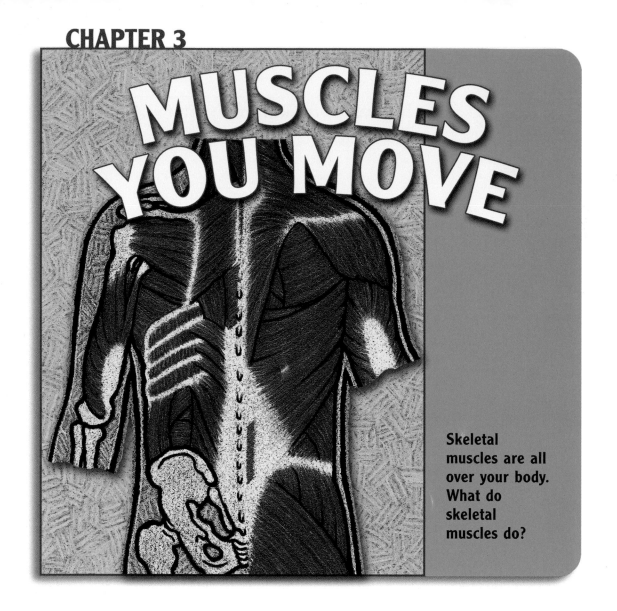

Skeletal muscles are all over your body. What do skeletal muscles do?

You have three different kinds of muscles in your body. All three kinds are made up of muscle fibers that contract. But each kind of muscle does a special job.

Muscles that you control are called skeletal muscles. The biceps is a skeletal muscle. Skeletal muscles have long, thin muscle fibers. Under a microscope, the fibers look striped.

Skeletal muscle cells look like a bunch of striped straws bundled together.

Most skeletal muscles are attached to bones. When the muscles contract, they pull on the bones where they are attached. Your bones cannot move without the help of muscles.

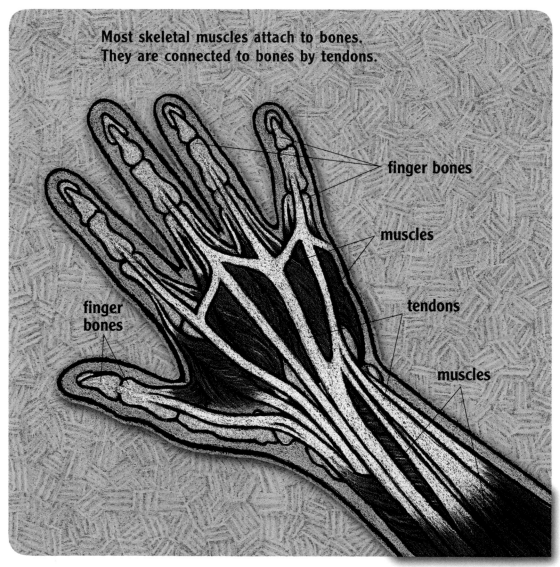

Most skeletal muscles attach to bones. They are connected to bones by tendons.

finger bones

muscles

finger bones

tendons

muscles

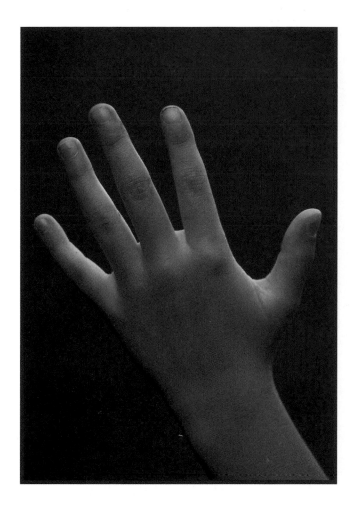

**Tendons connect muscles to bones. Wiggle your fingers. You can see your tendons move.**

Tendons connect muscles to bones. Look at the back of your hand. Try wiggling your fingers. Do you see the cords moving just under your skin? Those cords are tendons. They connect muscles in your lower arm to your finger bones.

No bone can move without the help of a muscle. But muscles can only pull. They cannot push. That's why many skeletal muscles come in pairs. One muscle pulls a bone in one direction. Then the other muscle pulls the bone in the opposite direction.

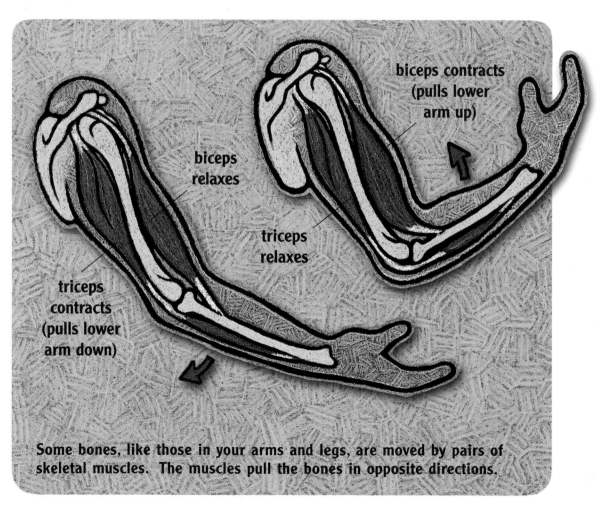

biceps contracts
(pulls lower
arm up)

biceps
relaxes

triceps
relaxes

triceps
contracts
(pulls lower
arm down)

Some bones, like those in your arms and legs, are moved by pairs of skeletal muscles. The muscles pull the bones in opposite directions.

**Your biceps and triceps muscles pull in opposite directions to move your lower arm up and down.**

In your upper arm, your biceps is paired with a muscle called the triceps (TRY-sehps). These muscles are attached to bones in your lower arm and your shoulder. When your biceps contracts, your lower arm is pulled up. When your triceps contracts, your lower arm is pulled down.

**Hundreds of muscles are used in complex movements.**

Most movements need more than just two muscles. More than three hundred muscles work together when you take a single step!

Not all skeletal muscles are attached only to bones. Some are attached to other muscles. Some are attached to skin.

Skeletal muscles attached to skin on your face can raise an eyebrow. Others can pull the corners of your mouth up into a smile.

**Many skeletal muscles in your face are attached to your skin. Nearly one-fourth of all the skeletal muscles in your body are in your face.**

Skeletal muscles come in all sorts of shapes and sizes. Big fan-shaped muscles are in your chest. They help move your arms at the shoulder. A flat sheet of muscle is just under your rib cage. It changes the shape of your chest to help you breathe.

**Many skeletal muscles are large and powerful. They help you make big body movements.**

**Calf muscles in your lower legs help you run.**

Your calf muscles are some of the strongest muscles in your body. They help you jump, walk, and run.

The many different muscles in your legs help you move your legs in many different ways.

Your longest skeletal muscles are on the inside of your legs. They stretch from your hips to the insides of your knees. Thanks to these muscles, you can sit cross-legged!

There are about 20 small muscles in your hands.  With their help, you can make a fist.  Or you can play the piano.  Or you can pick up a dime.

**Smaller, less powerful skeletal muscles control body parts that move in small ways.**

Six muscles move each of your eyes. These muscles allow you to look in many directions. Keep your head still and look around. You can feel your eye muscles at work.

**Six muscles control the movement of each eyeball.**

When skeletal muscles contract over and over again, they quickly get tired. They need to rest before they can work again.

Skeletal muscles are powerful. But when they are working hard, they get tired quickly. Try squeezing a small rubber ball over and over again. Soon the muscles in your hand will start to hurt.

After a while, you won't be able to squeeze the ball even one more time. Your muscles are too tired to contract. Stop squeezing. Let the muscles in your hand rest. Soon they will be ready to work again.

# CHAPTER 4

# MUSCLES THAT MOVE THEMSELVES

Smooth muscle is in blood vessels. Can you control smooth muscle?

The second kind of muscle in your body is smooth muscle. Unlike skeletal muscle, you can't control smooth muscle. Smooth muscle contracts automatically. It contracts all by itself. That way, you don't have to think about things like digesting your food!

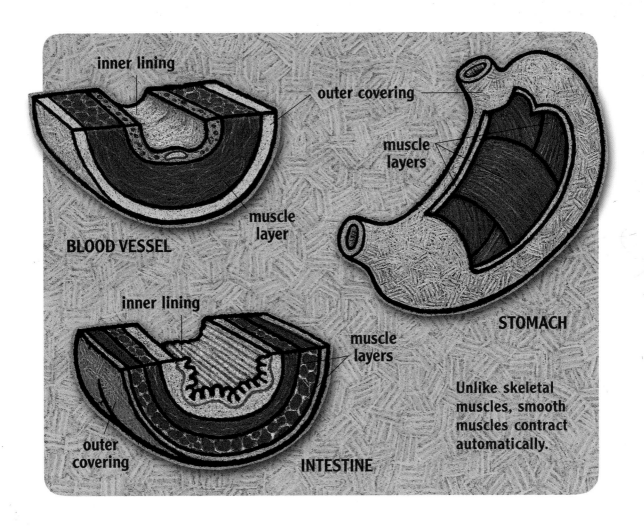

inner lining

outer covering

muscle layers

muscle layer

**BLOOD VESSEL**

**STOMACH**

inner lining

muscle layers

outer covering

**INTESTINE**

Unlike skeletal muscles, smooth muscles contract automatically.

Smooth muscle is found in the walls of your stomach. It is found in your blood vessels. It also makes up part of many organs in your body. When you are cold, tiny smooth muscles pull on the hairs in your skin. You get goose bumps!

Under a microscope, smooth muscle fibers look different from skeletal muscle fibers. They work differently too. Skeletal muscles can contract very fast. But smooth muscles contract slowly and steadily.

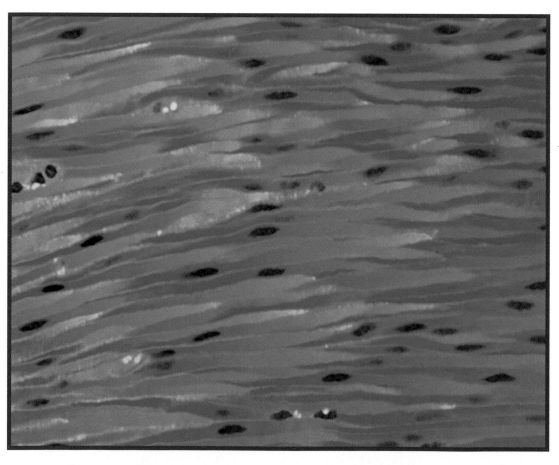

Smooth muscle fibers are pointed at the ends. They don't have stripes like skeletal muscle fibers do.

Your stomach can hold a lot of food because the smooth muscles in the stomach wall can stretch.

Smooth muscles are often arranged in flat sheets. A sheet of smooth muscle can stretch a lot! The smooth muscles in your stomach stretch so your stomach can hold a big meal.

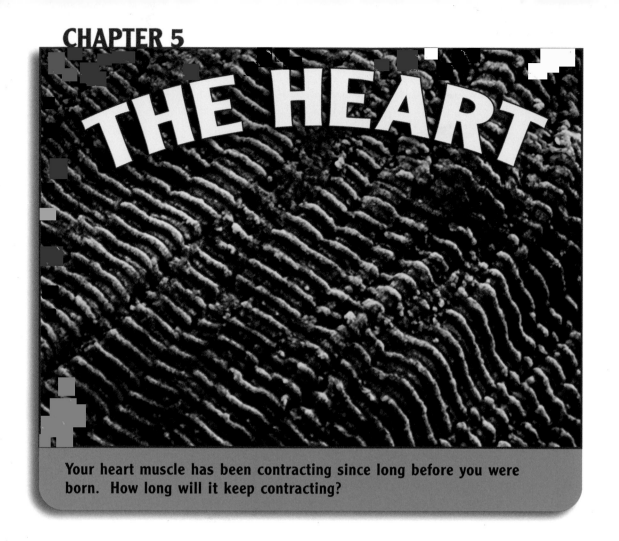

# CHAPTER 5

# THE HEART

Your heart muscle has been contracting since long before you were born.  How long will it keep contracting?

The third kind of muscle in your body is heart muscle.  Heart muscle is found only in the walls of your heart.  You can't control heart muscle.  It contracts automatically.  That's a good thing.  You wouldn't want to have to think about every heartbeat!

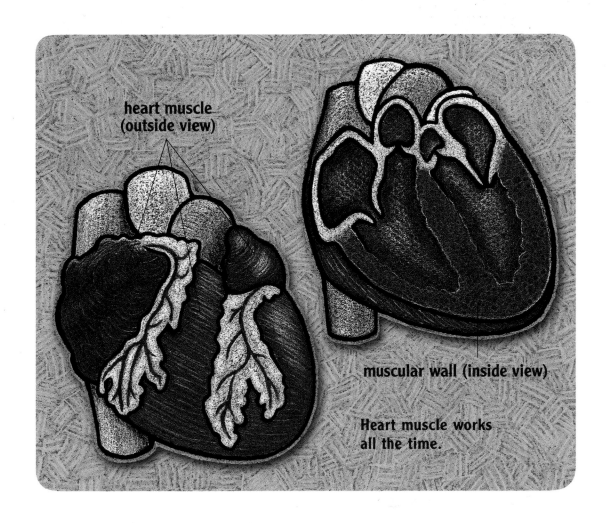

heart muscle
(outside view)

muscular wall (inside view)

Heart muscle works
all the time.

Under a microscope, heart muscle looks a
little bit like skeletal muscle. But it's different in
an important way. Heart muscle never gets
tired. It contracts about 70 times every minute.
That's about 100,000 times a day. Heart muscle
never rests during your entire life.

Put your hand on the left side of your chest. Can you feel a thumping? That's your heart beating. With each beat, your powerful heart muscle contracts.

Your heart makes a lub-dub, lub-dub sound as it beats. Your doctor listens to these heart sounds when you get a checkup.

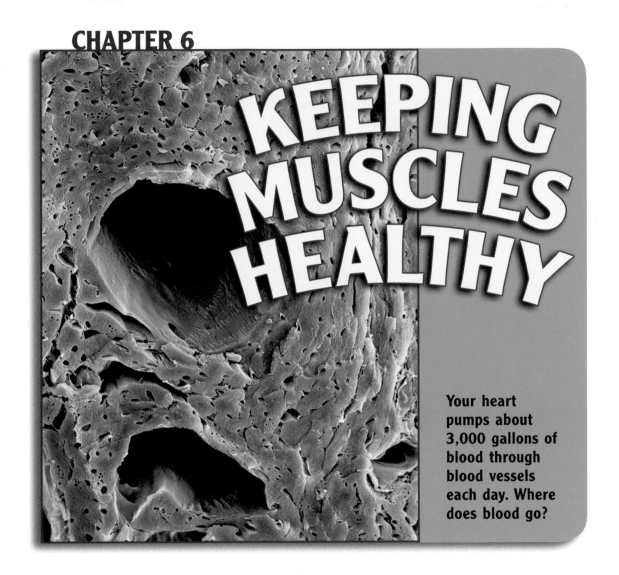

# CHAPTER 6

# KEEPING MUSCLES HEALTHY

Your heart pumps about 3,000 gallons of blood through blood vessels each day. Where does blood go?

Each time your heart muscle contracts, it pumps blood out of your heart. The blood is pumped through your body. Blood carries nutrients to your body's cells. Nutrients feed cells. Some of those cells are muscle fibers.

**Food gives your body the nutrients it needs.**

Your body's cells need nutrients to work
well. Nutrients come from the food you eat.
Eating well helps keep your muscles healthy.

Blood also carries oxygen to your cells. You
bring oxygen into your body with every breath.
The harder your muscles work, the more oxygen
they need.

Hard work is good for muscles. Exercise doesn't give you more muscles. But the muscles you have get bigger and stronger.

**When you exercise hard, you breathe faster and more deeply. This brings more oxygen into your body.**

Without exercise, muscles shrink. They lose their strength. Think about when you've been sick in bed for a long time. When you first start to walk again, your muscles feel weak.

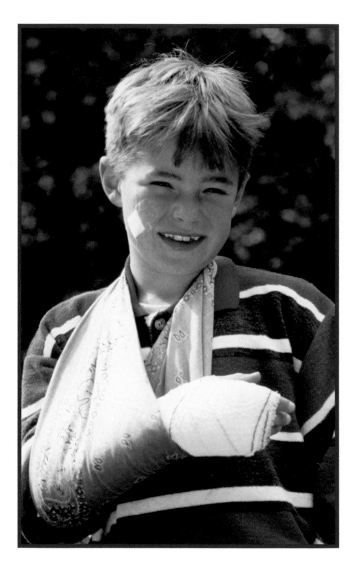

When your arm is in a cast, you can't use your muscles. They get weak.

**Your muscles work around the clock to keep you alive and healthy. They even work when you're asleep!**

You probably don't think much about your muscles. But whether you're asleep or awake, your muscles are always working. At any one time, some muscles are contracting. Other muscles are relaxing. But they are all working together. Muscles make your body move in just the right way.

# ON SHARING A BOOK

When you share a book with a child, you show that reading is important. To get the most out of the experience, read in a comfortable, quiet place. Turn off the television and limit other distractions, such as telephone calls.

Be prepared to start slowly. Take turns reading parts of this book. Stop occasionally and discuss what you're reading. Talk about the photographs. If the child begins to lose interest, stop reading. When you pick up the book again, revisit the parts you have already read.

## BE A VOCABULARY DETECTIVE

The word list on page 5 contains words that are important in understanding the topic of this book. Be word detectives and search for the words as you read the book together. Talk about what the words mean and how they are used in the sentence. Do any of these words have more than one meaning? You will find the words defined in a glossary on page 46.

## WHAT ABOUT QUESTIONS?

Use questions to make sure the child understands the information in this book. Here are some suggestions:

> What did this paragraph tell us? What does this picture show? What do you think we'll learn about next? Why do you need muscles in your body? What muscles can you move by thinking about them? What muscles move on their own? What can you do to keep your muscles healthy? What is your favorite part of the book? Why?

If the child has questions, don't hesitate to respond with questions of your own, such as What do you think? Why? What is it that you don't know? If the child can't remember certain facts, turn to the index.

## INTRODUCING THE INDEX

The index helps readers find information without searching through the whole book. Turn to the index on page 48. Choose an entry such as *tendons* and ask the child to use the index to find out what tendons do. Repeat with as many entries as you like. Ask the child to point out the differences between an index and a glossary. (The index helps readers find information, while the glossary tells readers what words mean.)

# FURTHER READING/WEBSITES

## LEARN MORE ABOUT
## THE MUSCULAR SYSTEM

### BOOKS

LeVert, Suzanne. *Bones and Muscles.* New York: Benchmark Books, 2002. Learn how muscles and bones work together.

O'Brien-Palmer, Michelle. *Watch Me Grow: Fun Ways to Learn about Cells, Bones, Muscles, and Joints.* Chicago: Chicago Review Press, 1999. This science activity book explores the muscles, bones, and joints and the cells they are made of, where all growth really takes place.

Simon, Seymour. *Muscles: Our Muscular System.* New York: HarperCollins, 1998. Shows and describes our muscles and their functions, as well as the effect of exercise.

Treays, Rebecca. *Understanding Your Muscles and Bones.* Tulsa, OK: EDC Publications, 1997. Gives facts about muscles and bones.

### WEBSITES

Pathfinders for Kids: The Muscular System—The Bundles of Energy
<http://infozone.imcpl.org/kids_musc.htm>
This web page has a list of resources you can use to learn more about the muscular system.

Your Gross and Cool Body—Muscular System
<http://yucky.kids.discovery.com/flash/body/pg000123.html>
This website includes some muscle facts and links to learning about other body functions.

Your Multi-Talented Muscles
<http://www.kidshealth.org/kid/body/muscles_noSW.html>
This fun website has information on the muscular system, links to other body systems, movies, games, and activities.

# GLOSSARY

**biceps (BYE-sehps):** the muscle on the front of your upper arm

**blood vessels:** the tubes in the body that carry blood

**brain:** a complex organ in the head that controls all body processes

**cells:** the smallest building blocks of body structures

**contract:** to shorten or pull together

**heart muscle:** the muscle in the heart. It contracts automatically.

**microscope:** a tool that makes very small things look bigger

**muscle fiber:** a muscle cell

**nerves:** cells that carry messages between the brain and the rest of the body

**nutrients (NOO-tree-ehnts):** food for your cells

**organs:** body parts that have a special purpose. The lungs, stomach, liver, and brain are organs.

**oxygen:** a gas that all cells need, carried in the blood

**skeletal muscle:** muscle that you move

**smooth muscle:** muscle that contracts automatically

**tendons:** tough bands that connect muscles to bones

**triceps (TRY-sehps):** the muscle on the back of your upper arm

# INDEX

Pages listed in **bold** type refer to photographs.